IBERIAN VILLAGES

NORMAN F CARVER JR

Books by Norman F. Carver, Jr.:

FORM AND SPACE OF JAPANESE ARCHITECTURE
SILENT CITIES, MEXICO AND THE MAYA
ITALIAN HILLTOWNS

IBERIAN VILLAGES

PORTUGAL & SPAIN

NORMAN F CARVER JR

DOCUMAN PRESS

ACKNOWLEDGEMENTS

This work has extended over more than a decade and during that time many persons have given me assistance and advice. I cannot remember them all. My deepest gratitude must go to the many Portugese and Spaniards who never resented my intrusions, and were always friendly and helpful. I should especially like to thank, in Lisbon, Tama, Milu, and Carl who not only directed me to some outstanding villages in Portugal, but took me in when I returned exhausted from my travels. At various times, my son Norman III, my daughter Cristina, and my wife all accompanied me. My thanks to them for their companionship and their patience while I climbed a hill for a long view or waited hours for the right light or went without meals in the desire to use every minute of a fading sun. In the preparation of the book, Harry Randall again gave much invaluable advice and editorial help. Roger Hansen skillfully made hundreds of proof prints. The printers, and especially Rolf Hammer worked diligently and skillfully under a difficult schedule to achieve the desired results.

Again my wife, Joan, contributed endlessly to the project at every stage and without her help it could never have been completed.

Documan Press, Ltd.
Post Office Box 387
Kalamazoo, Michigan 49005

ISBN: 0-932976-02-5 cloth
ISBN: 0-932976-02-3 paper

Designed by Norman F. Carver, Jr.
Printed by EPI, Inc.
Battle Creek, Michigan
Printed in the United States

*For my mother and father, whose high
creative standards were an inspiration.*

CONTENTS

PREFACE

Almost from the beginning, man has made two kinds of architecture. Foremost has always been the architecture of the monuments, temples, and palaces. Built in one of the recognized styles such as Greek, Roman, Gothic, or Modern, this high-style architecture had its own refined aesthetic and palette of acceptable forms. These are the structures so thoroughly documented in the authoritative histories of architecture (whose comprehensiveness may be judged by their failure to include any building east of Egypt). But, as influential as these buildings have been, they are only a tiny fraction of the built environment.

It is the second kind of architecture, those plain, unassuming dwellings in which man has lived over the centuries, that comprises the overwhelming mass of buildings. This is folk or vernacular architecture. In contrast with the pretensions, heroics, and esoteric aesthetics of high-style architecture, its primary motivation was practical, economical shelter. Anonymous craftsmen, disregarding the dominant historical styles, developed forms reflecting the local climate, sites, materials, and needs. Hence vernacular aesthetics sprang from the materials and the construction process itself rather than from imposed abstract concepts. Until very recently, these common and unpretentious structures were largely dismissed as unsophisticated and unimportant.

What is their importance? In ITALIAN HILLTOWNS, the first book in this series, I discussed vernacular architecture's significance as well as its general characteristics in some detail. I will not repeat that discussion here except to stress that indigenous architecture is perhaps our only chance to see some of the fundamental connections between man, society, the natural environment, and architecture. Simpler societies ignored these relationships at their peril. But, shielded by modern technology and obscured by complex functional needs as well as by centuries of stylistic indulgence, these fundamental relationships are now often ignored. The result is a contemporary architecture that is often ecologically unsound and remote from reality.

IBERIAN VILLAGES presents an architecture that not only reflects many of these relationships but does it with elan. It is an architecture that re-affirms the universality of certain vernacular characteristics first outlined in ITALIAN HILLTOWNS. Such characteristics are by their very universality "a basis for a language of form and the means by which we can retain our continuity with the past and enrich our future". The characteristics of vernacular are:

1. Forms are functionally motivated in the fullest sense --that is, physically and psychologically.

2. They are precisely adapted to climate and environment.

3. They reflect the building process and local skills, materials, and technology.

4. They are produced by the whole community and share a common tradition.

5. They vary in detail but seldom in type.

6. Ornamentation, if it is used, generally grows out of the solution to some functional problem.

7. The repetitive individual house form is transcended by the vivid and unique overall form of the whole village.

8. Growth is slow, open-ended, and always in human scale.

ORIGINS OF IBERIAN FORMS

There is an underlying similarity to much of the architecture in the Mediterranean basin, reflecting not only a fairly uniform environment but thousands of years of cultural interchange fostered by this convenient sea road. In fact, Mediterranean vernacular can be seen as variations on one main theme --dense hilltowns of stone sheltered against the sun and marauders from the sea.

Iberia --wild and remote at the uncharted end of the Sea -- had little contact with the rest of the civilized world until late Roman times. This remoteness, together with extremes of climate and geography within Iberia and the settlement by culturally diverse groups over the centuries, has produced an astonishing variety of dwellings and village forms.

As in many cultures, the immediate demands of site, climate and available materials, rather than subtler social needs, had the most obvious influence on folk forms. Iberian vernacular confirms this by the many examples where one group evolved various solutions to cope with different environments -- and conversely by the development of similar forms in similar environments by unrelated groups. Such clear reflection of environmental forces does not deny cultural influence, but it does confirm their usually more subtle effects.

One of these forces, climate, influenced the shape and orientation not only of individual houses but of whole villages. The grouping, orientation, number and size of openings, and the location of sleeping, cooking, and animal quarters were the only available means to moderate the climate --whether it was the baking heat of summer or the damp cold of winter.

The Land

Iberian climate is both benevolent and cruel. The peninsula roughly divides into four geographic-climatic regions, ranging from the Alpine to the tropical. The northern region, tempered by the Atlantic, is cool and rainy with high, lush mountains in the interior reminiscent of Switzerland. Because of its remoteness and inaccessibility this region remained free of the Moslem conquest and it is from this enclave the reconquest of the south began. Galacia, in the very northwest corner of Spain, and northern Portugal, though less mountainous, have a similar climate.

In the central part of the peninsula lies the most typical and most influential region -- the high, arid plateaus and mountains of Castile and Extremadura. It is a land of bitterly cold winters and hot dry summers where, despite the impression of vast plains, one is never far from the mountains.

The eastern and southeastern coastal areas are a third region, semi-tropical and typically Mediterranean in feeling. Unfortunately it is the most corrupted by modernization, so little original architecture remains. Fourth is the southwest, stretching from Granada in Spain to the Portugese Atlantic Coast --a relatively hot, dry region of rugged terrain and also huge plains.

Tourist brochures to the contrary, the climate can be extreme in all areas. As the Spanish proverb says, "Nine months of winter and three months of hell".

Iberian Origins

In coping with these extremes early settlers used construction techniques which they brought with them. These were as basic as

7

AN INTRODUCTION TO IBERIA

Centuries of strife on the Iberian peninsula caused
widespread building of fortified hilltowns — towns
where the houses clustered around a castle on some
strategic peak. Such towns were built by Moslems
defending their shrinking frontier or by Christian
lords resisting attacks from Moors or rival lords.

Almansa's (9) Moorish citadel emerges from a rock
that rises abruptly out of the plains of La Mancha.
Alcala (10) is a northern town in the high mountains
near Teruel. The southern town of Monte Frio,
dominated by its fortress-like church, is built around a
defendable rock to which the inhabitants could retire
when under attack (11, 178-183).

The dispersed, sun-seeking houses of Carmona (12, 49-51), a northern mountain village, contrast with the densely packed sun-shielding houses in the southern hilltown of Casares. (13, 152-161).

Compact towns with narrow streets occur in both the north and south but the atmosphere is entirely different. The southern streets are clean, bright, inviting and an integral part of the town's structure. On the other hand, some northern streets, nearly sealed off by projecting upper stories, seem merely left-over, utilitarian passages.

La Alberca a northern mountain town (14, 78-91). Vejer de la Frontera (15, 144-145).

Frequent features of northern towns are the arcaded streets or plazas. The porticos shade inhabitants from the hot sun, shelter them from rain, and expand their main floor work spaces. Porticos also permit expansion of the upper stories and are the location for weekly markets in many towns. The portico is a different kind of space, neither indoors nor out, but a transition between.

La Alberca's medieval main square has arcades on three sides (16, 78-91). This stepped portico leads off the square at Penaranda de Duero (17, 66-67).

The casual blending of column styles with slightly
irregular arches introduces variety within the portico's
ordered rhythms. A disadvantage — the darkening of
the lower floor — is mitigated in Garovillas (19, 94-96)
by the use of thin columns and whitewash that reflects
the light deep inside, unlike the somber porticos
around the plaza in Horta de San Juan (18).

One of the southern village's most appealing aspects is the wave-like pattern of tiled roofs seen from above. The traditional tile roofs are a rich texture of variegated earthtones that combine handsomely with the white walls beneath. This stunning complex at Castellar near Algeciras incorporates subtle curves and the patina of great age. Unfortunately, these roofs are being replaced with modern tiles of a uniform and harsh orange color.

A building form that appears unique to Iberia (but occurs elsewhere in Europe and Asia) is the raised storage house, called in Spanish 'horrero'. Raising the building on pillars with flat stone caps protects the contents from rats and moisture. Stone horreros, such as these at Lindoso (24, 33-34), are common in the northwest of Spain and Portugal. The wooden types are found throughout the northern mountains of the peninsula. This (22-23) is near Cangas de Onis.

the Visigoth's north European wooden huts, as structurally advanced as the Roman arch, and as environmentally sound as the Moorish courtyard --though sometimes adapted to conditions inconsistent with their origins. Little remains of the earliest Iberian and later Celtic or Visigoth settlements. Evidently they lived in archetypal hilltop *castros*, collections of stone or wood huts and animal pens ringed with moats and rubble walls.

The Romans were the first to attempt to unify the unruly tribes of the peninsula. During the first to the fifth centuries they attempted to break up the clan system by moving people from small remote, hilltop hamlets into valley towns connected by an extensive system of roads. The road network was an effective means of unification that lasted for centuries. But it also permanently by-passed many places, leaving them more isolated and forgotten than ever. Beyond roads, bridges, and aqueducts, the Romans also left their mark in the characteristic grid plans of their civic centers, many of which still exist as the cores of modern cities.

Roman colonists devised the pattern of large estates under absentee owners who lived in the towns off the profits of their land holdings. The pattern persists to this day especially in the south. With the collapse of the Roman Empire and the subsequent invasions of the Visigoths and Vandals in the fifth century, A.D. an Iberian 'dark age' began. It was a a period of stagnation that, except for a few primitive churches, left little behind.

Islam

In the first half of the eighth century southern and central Iberia was rapidly occupied by Moslem invaders from North Africa. Since Spain and Portugal did not exist as political entities, but as a collection of independent kingdoms whose only common tie was their Christianity, the Moslems were able to occupy most of the peninsula within forty years and set up a strong central government for the first time since the Romans. The Moslem occupation initiated a decisive period in Iberian history, unleashing forces of accord and divisiveness that have racked the peninsula ever since.

The Moors never conquered all, however. In the far north the fierce mountain people held out in their ancient *castros* and from here the re-conquest began --slowly but inexorably moving south until the last Moslem ruler retreated from Granada to a small enclave in the Sierra Nevada. They were finally expelled by King Ferdinand and Queen Isabella in the same year that Columbus discovered America. Moslem control, though diminishing in extent, lasted 700 years.

The centuries of struggle that began in the remote mountains of the north no doubt added to that region's especially strong separatist attitudes. Such attitudes spread as various sections of the peninsula were reconquered and emerged as small independent kingdoms. In Spain the reconquest proceeded slowly and erratically, creating stubborn pockets of resistance and liberation often separated from each other for centuries, and reinforcing a regional rivalry that still plagues Spain today. On the other hand, most of what is now Portugal gained a measure of freedom from Moslem rule as early as 1143, and, except for a brief period, has remained independent ever since.

Since the Christians fought among themselves as much as against the Moslems, central and southern Spain has literally hundreds of castles --from which the province of Castile derives its name. The effect of this rivalry was crippling. It hindered free trade and sapped manpower and energy away from maintaining the increased agricultural productivity that had developed under the Moors --"the battle against the Moors was won but the battle against nature was lost"[1].

Counteracting separatism was the unifying effect of the early Roman road network, the spread of Christianity, and the foreign influences along the coasts and along the great pilgrimage route to the shrine church at Santiago de Campostela. The *camino de Santiago* was the route for hundreds of thousands of pilgrims from all parts of Europe. It extended across northern Spain from the Pyrenees to the Atlantic coast. Entire villages along it were devoted to the pilgrims' needs (42-45).

The correlation between a society's built forms and its environment are especially evident in Iberia and specific examples will be examined in more detail in the discussion of each region. In general, geographically and culturally separated, each group developed its own methods and forms. Any impetus for change was through the normal evolution of needs and skills as well as through an evolving hierarchy of values and beliefs that changed priorities --and only occasionally through an extraordinary event such as outside contact or conquest.

Isolation and the strength of tradition are particularly evident in remote mountain regions of the north, where some very primitive dwellings were still in use until very recently (46-48). These basic, almost prehistoric forms show little effect from even so radical and durable an influence as the 700-year reign of the Moors -- strong evidence that, when the conservative countryside created a viable custom, it was not easily diverted. One reason for abandoning these ancient patterns so readily today is that modern technology and materials offer vast improvements in physical comfort and convenience. The desirability and availability of these conveniences together with the disappearance of traditional skills make radical change inevitable.

Though even in lonely places change was inevitable, the subsistence level of many early societies did not encourage idle experimentation or frivolous embellishments. While discouragement of innovation insured continuity and order in the community by avoiding the arbitrary or merely fashionable, it also prevented needed improvements.

Country versus City

Though change is a constant in any society, it is the rate at which a society is forced to absorb the new that determines whether it can retain its integrity. Small communities regulated their rate of change and their internal order informally through recognized customs. As municipalities grew in size and complexity, a more rigid and formal system of laws was required. This in turn weakened the sense of participation and the shared value system that is the essence of any tradition --hastening its demise.

In the villages it was relatively easy for time-honored rules and an all-powerful aristocracy to control life, but in the city a measure of independence was possible and the customs were more flexible. This undermined the established order and eventually affected rural life as well. Unrestrained by small town mores, the cities quickly adopted the latest fashions, new ideas, and foreign influences, while the countryside remained conservative and suspicious, accepting new ideas grudgingly if at all.

There has always been a love-hate relationship between city and country. It has existed in nearly every culture, ancient or modern. Country folk, even while longing for the riches and freedom of the cities, regarded life there as physically unhealthy and morally corrupting. City dwellers, in turn, secretly longed for the return to the simpler, purer life of the countryside and the village.

But the pure life was a hard life, a constant struggle to survive against the ravages of nature, marauding armies, and overbearing and feuding landlords. For most people the city was the only opportunity for escape to a life of greater ease, prosperity and security. It was an opportunity they seized with eternal regret for the life they, or their ancestors, had left behind.

The Spaniard, particularly, is susceptible to this emotional tug; he feels little loyalty to anyone except his family and his village. Such fierce local pride, bred in centuries of insularity, has been the source of much of the conflict in Spanish history.

Today the problem is how to exploit the very real advantages of new technology and methods while maintaining the equally real but more subtle and ordinary values of the past. Especially in Spain, which is modernizing at a furious pace, little thought has been given to preservation. Portugal's Monsaraz (106-116) is an admirable exception. By contrast, Italy has several examples of the successful integration of ancient forms and modern amenities such as

Siena and San Gimignano.

Image and Meaning

Many Iberian villages are visually compelling --at least for the casual visitor. It might seem that most inhabitants would have become oblivious to the visual attractions of their native place. But it is difficult to believe that a native of Olvera (135-137), for example, as he glanced back at his village from the fields nearby, could fail to be stirred. Olvera's image is brilliant and potent --at once unique, familiar and orderly. Moreover, it was the center of the inhabitant's universe and it symbolized the established order by the intimate scale of the repetitive, anonymous cottages nestled in the natural contours of the site dominated by the hovering mass of the church or castle. It was a geometry at once integrated with and distinct from the landscape which sustained it --a form determined as much by nature as by man and his institutions. Communicated daily to the inhabitants over a lifetime, generation after generation, it is an image of man, nature, and God in consort and conflict.

Mirroring reality the image could not be trivial. The more remote they were, the more important this image was in the inhabitants' view of themselves and their culture. "The environment men create through their wants becomes a mirror that reflects their civilization; more importantly it also constitutes a book in which is written the formula of life that they communicate to others and transmit to succeeding generations. The characteristics of the environment are therefore of importance not only because they affect the comfort and quality of present-day life, but even more because they condition the development of young people and thereby society..."[2]

Order and Form

Except for their central plazas most villages developed without any preconceived plans or deliberate vistas and compositions. In Spain, an excessive individualism -the attitude of *viva yo* (hurray for me) --made nearly impossible the conception, let alone the execution, of grand schemes. Abstract concepts requiring systematic planning were anathema to the Spaniard more concerned with immediate results.

In place of planning the accidental, expedient clustering of structures created ever changing asymmetries full of surprising views, picturesque juxtapositions of forms, and varied spaces. The consistency and order of the village derived, not from abstract concepts, but from a shared value system that insured an underlying consistency at the same time allowing limited variations of the parts to fit individual needs. Conformity to the deep rooted 'way' was expected and required.

Still insular conformity was relatively lax when contrasted with the rigid geometries of high-style planning where concepts were often adopted more for their novelty and elite aesthetics than for their practicality. Vernacular, while it sometimes discouraged needed change, was at least based on the realities of its locale. It was this foundation which enabled a tradition to act as an "invisible hand" guiding the parts towards a unified and ordered whole even as it grew by accretion --adapting to needs and opportunities without any formal overall conception.

Coherence and regularity came from working within the accepted palette of materials, scale, color, and shapes in fashioning individual dwellings. In addition, common sense oriented individual houses into similar directions even on rugged sites --for example, with entrances and windows facing away from cold winds and towards the sun. Hillside sites with streets necessarily parallel to the slope also imposed a uniform orientation --an aesthetic and practical advantage when the town was built on the south slope (13, 158, 172, 180).

Essential to maintaining a sense of order was a limited scale so that the connection of man-made with natural forms was never lost or the irregular pattern of streets and houses did not become endless and overwhelming to the individual. By contrast, the changes now occurring are especially disruptive, since they involve rapid change in scale and unrestrained growth --as well as unfamiliar materials and technology.

Deadly uniformity was prevented by the adaptation of the elemental dwelling to fit varying family needs or irregular sites, and by individual expression in minor and decorative details. The composition was also unbounded; it could be added to without 'spoiling' the conception by extending the underlying functional network of connecting spaces.The only limits were the constraints of enclosing walls or precipitous sites. In any case the edges of the urban areas were clearly defined -- additions were always adjacent to existing structures. Limited means, then, gave the villages an inherent unity, while exploiting these means created practical, complex, and visually rich environments --without destroying that unity.

Reading Forms

The village forms can, of course, be read on several levels. First, especially from a distance, they can be viewed as abstract sculptural forms with their own aesthetic coherence and fit with the landscape.

Then, as one moves into and through a town, the dominant sense is of a functioning organism structured to meet the inhabitants' needs for shelter, work, and social intercourse.

The surface uniformity soon dissolves. As the houses, churches, castles, streets and plazas are examined, one sees that each element is unique --especially the dwellings whose scale, asymmetry, and flexibility allow endless combinations. Churches, on the other hand, as ceremonial spaces and as pervasive symbols of power, are grand in scale, symmetrical and set apart from the mass of anonymous cottages. Similarly, castles, in addition to their defensive function contribute to the distinctive silhouette of each village (9, 147-149).

Village Patterns

While there is little reliable data on the establishment of particular Iberian towns, the general pattern is discernable and familiar. As in Italy and throughout the Mediterranean, compact hilltop sites were chosen for protection against enemies, to preserve agricultural land, and as market centers for the surrounding countryside. Since all land was owned by the nobles, most of the towns were organized by fiat to resettle and defend areas captured from the retreating Moors. The kings issued *fueros* or charters that granted special freedoms to many of them. As these free centers gained in economic importance, their independence attracted increasing numbers escaping from the poverty of the countryside and the oppression of petty local nobility.

Thus the location and growth of municipalities was determined by a complex interrelationship of accident, political and military needs, land ownership, climate, availability of good sites with a plentiful water supply, and agricultural potential. While the totality of forces is complex, the powerful effects of climate, water, and fertility of the land are readily apparent. For example, the wet northern area with its fertile valleys and good water permitted individual land ownership with people living on or close to their small plots. Villages, therefore, are numerous and small -- sometimes mere agglomerations of farm houses (49-51).

The long dry periods in much of the land made water supply a critical factor in the establishment of a town. Lack of water also limited the ability of individual families to survive on remote farms and forced cooperative efforts in agriculture, such as irrigation. As a result, the country towns in dry areas with good soil are typically large and widely dispersed on huge estates.

In dry areas with poorer soil, such as the central plateau, individual plots were also rare and large non-intensive farming, primarily olive groves or sheepherding, was the rule. Here long periods of inactivity alternating with short intensive harvests made the country towns a refuge much of the year and the only source of work at other times. They are rather large, generally poor, and infrequent.

Conditions, then, forced much of the populace into large villages dependent on the vast land holdings of one family. Since the sixteenth century there have been numerous attempts to break this feudal pattern by resettlement on unused agricultural land, but attitudes are so entrenched that the villages rather than independent farms remain the center of rural life.

STREET PATTERN, MEDINA AT CORDOBA

Additional factors were the differences between the Moslem and Christian areas, remnants of which still endure. "....... in Christian Spain local liberties and feudal privileges developed side by side, whilst among the Moslems nothing was permitted to infringe upon the powers of the central government. This history of Spain can thus be interpreted in the light of two different conceptions of land tenure. In the north the possession of land stood for profit and well being. In the former case the feudal idea became in time, through the medium of the free communes and the increase in the number of *mayorazgos* (entailed estates) democratized: even the humblest aspired to power, to nobility, to family permanence, and the result was a society in which the gentlemanly ideal of leisure and authority took precedence over that of material well being. In the latter a much more expansive and hedonistic frame of mind prevailed and work was regarded as the only road to prosperity."[3]

This attitude, often commented on by Spanish writers is reflected in the ideal of "the impoverished knight" who avoids regimentation and physical labor by escape to the city.

While there may not have been the extreme civic pride of the Italian city-states, citizenship in the Christian towns was a privilege. Citizenship in Moslem towns, all of them under a strong central government, was not a unique right.

Moslem towns also developed without any overall plan. Streets were a maze of narrow lanes lined with blank walled houses. The main public spaces around the mosques were the markets. The density and the customary sequestering of women and family from public life turned the houses inwards on their own courtyards and gardens. Even the smallest opened directly off the street into a small court, sometimes with a well or fountain and always with plants --a common feature to this day in the towns of the south (144-145).

Thus in Iberia three main factors influenced the character and siting of both individual houses and the villages: one, the physical realities --climate, water sources, construction materials, defense, and type of agriculture; two, the cultural influences --a feudal system with entrenched regional traditions; and three, perhaps as an outgrowth of the other two, the character of the people themselves --independent, loyal first to family and clan and with a tendency to avoid abstract, cooperative planning.

In addition, the individual's needs and wealth as well as the skills of local craftsmen introduced other variations. The results are an exceptional opportunity to examine the interplay between architecture, culture, and environment.

Spain and Portugal

The differences between Spanish and Portugese vernacular are differences in detail and 'style' not in type. There is, in fact, a remarkable correspondence in the native buildings of the two countries --just as geography and climate ignored the border so, roughly, did the architecture. In the north sections of both countries, for example, there is wide use of the *horrero* (22-24, 34-35), the wood or stone granaries raised on stilts. And proceeding south in both countries, the types and materials change in corresponding fashion --from the massive stone work of the north to the white stuccoed towns of the south.

NORTHERN IBERIA
PHOTOGRAPHS

The classic composition and heroic site of Morella makes it one of the most spectacular of Spain's walled towns. A site occupied since Iberian times, its mile long wall was begun in the early 14th century when it was one of a series of fortified towns on the Christian frontier. Later Morella was an outpost in conflicts between Valencia and Aragon and because of its strategic position has been repeatedly conquered or beseiged — last in 1873. The interior streets are narrow and winding with steep ramps and stairs where they ascend the rock but the original architecture is much changed.

At the village of Lindoso in northern Portugal, more than 50 stone graneries are grouped near the castle — for protection and the availability of flat stone outcroppings used as threshing floors (34, 22, 24).

The wooden horrero of northern Spain come in a variety of styles and frequently stand alongside the south-facing, balconied houses. Near Cangas (35).

Monsanto (36b, 37) is a curious town built among huge boulders that form part of the houses. The masonry in this area is a remarkable blend of rough textured walls and large smooth stones used structurally as lintels and jambs of openings or to strengthen corners. The apparently arbitrary shapes tie the stones into the wall and their expressiveness is frequently enhanced with whitewash. It is a splendid example of how ornamentation in vernacular architecture is so often functionally derived.

Windows near Braga (36t).

The twin doorways of a modest barn below Monsanto have the strength and dignity of an entrance to the tomb of some ancient king. Though working within a tradition, the mason was sensitive to the nuances of proportion and form in each stone and inventive in their assembly, thereby subtly transcending and transforming the tradition (38-39).

Country life in northern Portugal has changed little — these women are winnowing wheat on a threshing terrace high above a river valley near Guarda, much as they have for centuries. A sheepherder nearby displays his new charges. (40-41).

Penalba de Santiago (42-44). Penalba is a remote mountain village similar to many along the Camino de Santiago pilgrimage route that passed through these mountains. Roofs are of local slate and walls are of slabs of unmortared stone. Wood was sparingly used for roof structures and balconies — heavy snows and muddy streets made the balconies a necessity. Acebo, a tiny, lonely town whose only street was the Camino de Santiago, at one time was thronged with travelers. (45).

Penalba de Santiago

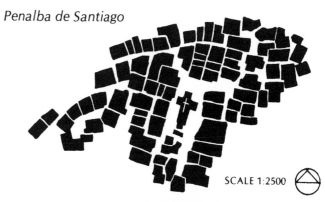

SCALE 1:2500

Huddled on the brow of a hill, sheltered against wind is this group of rare 'pallaza' houses, perhaps descended from prehistoric Iberian round houses, they were in use until a few years ago. They have been recently restored using many of the original furnishings. The simple furniture has carved decoration and a clever bench near the fire uses a tray that flips over the lap like a baby's high chair.

The center cross wall of the houses goes full height and supports the ends of the radiating roof rafters so the round or oval outer wall is a logical form. The interior is divided by this central wall into the animal and family areas with bedrooms sometimes above the animal barn. The interiors are dark, lit only by the open door and a few tiny windows. Cooking was over an open fire pit in the earthen floor and the smoke drifted up through the thatch.

El Cebrero, on the Camino de Santiago in provence of Galacia (46-48).

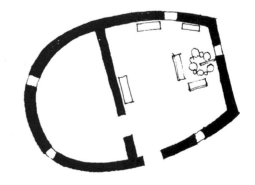

46

In marked contrast with the fortified hilltowns
further south, Carmona's site is a lush valley floor
adjacent to the terraced fields. This location and
Carmona's dispersed plan reflect a history of relative
security. Additional evidence of this vernacular
architecture's adaptation to its environment are the
houses themselves. They are loosely arranged in rows
that minimize exposed walls and orient the main
openings and balconies to the sun. In the wet, cold
climate balconies are essential outdoor space above
the mud and snow. Inside the large arches are the stair
to the living quarters above, storage for the family cart,
and pens for the animals — whose heat helps warm
the upper floor (49-51, 12).

Still very much in use, elevated wooden shoes
are a necessity in these muddy streets. Working under
the balcony of his house, the local shoemaker takes
about an hour to hand-carve a pair.

50

Frias, a hilltown above the beautiful Ebro River valley, guards a Roman bridge. Its castle hangs precariously from an elevated rock at the entrance to the town (52-53).

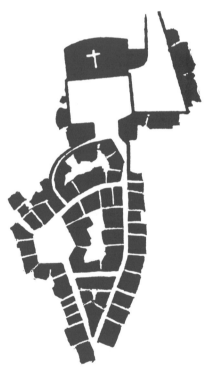

SCALE 1:2500

Its name a contraction of Saint Julliana, Santillana was a pilgrimage center in the Middle Ages, later an important seat of power, and now largely a farm community. Its history explains the rather grand style of some of its houses — mansions really, complete with coat of arms above the doors. Small and well preserved, Santillana is built along the few lanes leading to the monastery. Nearby are the Altamira caves. (54-58).

This entrance is just off the street in one of the larger mansions. The single classical column, an elegant gesture from Santillana's proud past, is remarkably effective in the midst of this rough hewn room and shows that the current fashion of mixing stylistically distant elements is not entirely original (56).

Arcade on Santillana's Plaza Mayor (58).

In compact northern towns the houses usually are without private court yards and so the many tiny plazas serve for leisurely gatherings in the sun. Batea (59).

Moorish arches form arcades and support the
upper floors of houses over the streets in Batea (60-61).

Two strikingly different techniques — half timber and stuccoed masonry are both used in the town of Goizueta and throughout the Basque region. The window treatment, similar to the elemental stonework of northern Portugal (36-39), seems however, more arbitrary and decorative set off by the white stucco that covers the underlying masonry (62-63).

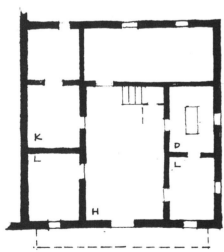

Vinuesa (64-65). This classic northern house has essentially the same layout as the simpler houses at Carmona (49-51) — though the cows and hay have been replaced by living rooms, dining room, and kitchen that open off the grand reception hall. A stairway at the back leads to sleeping rooms on the second floor.

A massive Renaissance palace and a delicate half-timbered house face each other on the Plaza Mayor in Penranda du Duero. This small country town was once an important defensive town along the Duero River that marked the limit of Moslem conquest in the north (66-68, 17).

An early Iberian site on a strategic hill, Segovia grew into a large walled town and the center of Castile's wool trade. Its impressive silhouette, punctuated by the towers of the great cathedral and the Alcazar, can be seen for great distances across the plains. Once occupied by Castilian kings, the castle, both in its form and its site on Segovia's prow is the most romantic in Spain (69-71).

Entrance to Pedraza, a sleepy, partially deserted Castilian town, is through a tiny gate in the outer wall and then along narrow streets leading to this handsome plaza partially enclosed by a variety of arcaded houses. The fading Arabic patterns of decorated stucco (73) are similar to those found in the mountains of Extremadura (91), a hundred miles to the West.

No matter how poor the village or how primitive its construction it has a kind of order imposed by the unity of materials and house forms and, not least, by the dominance of the omnipresent church. (Valbona 74).

Built over the edge of the cliff, these eight and ten story buildings on Cuenca's outer rim stretch the capability of wall bearing construction to its limits. Entrances are at the middle level on the street side (75).

The pressure for building space on Cuenca's cliff top forced houses to the very brink and beyond. These unusual and delicate wooden structures, the hanging houses of Cuenca have a distinct oriental flavor though the details are thoroughly Spanish (76-77).

The towns in the mountains of western Spain were long isolated, retaining a medieval flavor unlike any other region in Iberia. Premier among them for the authenticity of its atmosphere is La Alberca (79-90, 14), now protected from change by government controls.

Set in the midst of the wooded uplands, La Alberca has much the same character as its neighbor, Miranda del Castanar (78) whose jubilant roofscape gives little hint of somber streets below.

La Alberca's Plaza Publica (79-84) is surrounded with arcades on three sides off which are shops, the village offices, the tiny jail, and above, important houses. There are other small plazas and a larger space adjacent to the church, but the Plaza Publica is the focus of all activity. Everyone in the village will pass through here at least once a day and usually gather here in the evenings — on rainy evenings standing in groups under the porticos. And on festival days the plaza and the balconies are crowded with townspeople and visitors.

*In these dark, confining streets one is always
drawn towards the light and openness of the plaza.*

The houses follow a timeless pattern — storage and animal quarters on the first floor, sleeping rooms on the second, and the top floor for kitchen and living areas. Sometimes this upper floor has a small balcony opening onto the narrow street or a back yard. On a stone slab in the kitchen is a constantly smoldering fire that blackens the whole upper story before the smoke escapes through the cracks or chimney. Because it has the only access to light and air, the top floor is the most livable in these crowded towns; however, it means all firewood and food must be hauled up the steep stairs (85).

The building method is timber frame with an in-fill of rubble usually plastered over. The floors are framed with logs, covered with twigs and then a thick layer of smooth plaster. The house on page 85 reveals the full range of materials and techniques.

The portico on the east side of the Plaza, (84).

The three and four story houses are tightly packed, not for lack of space since there is no physical restriction to expansion (either natural or man-made), but because of a real or felt need for security and for the benefits of mutual structural support of the multi-story construction.

SCALE 1:2500

In this combination of stone, heavy timber and
plaster construction, each material is appropriately
used — stone as a massive base on the damp ground,
wood to span the longer horizontal spaces, and
plaster to seal against rain and drafts. The plaster
is occasionally incised with geometric patterns and
painted soft colors reminiscent of Arab designs in
the Alhambra at Granada. La Alberca (90) and nearby
Monforte (91).

Sheep have been both the blessing and the curse of Iberia — even while huge fortunes were made in the valuable wool trade, the over grazing caused irreparable damage to vast stretches of the dry central plateau. Originally grazing rights were granted to orders of knights on the abandoned lands between the Christian and Moslem frontier in exchange for its defense. Developing into the Mesta, the powerful guild of sheep owners extended and maintained absolute grazing rights for over five hundred years.

At its height, more than a million sheep swept across these plateaus in their annual passage from winter pasture in Castile and Extremadura to the summer pasture in the northern mountains. Rights of passage were absolute from which no farm or crop was safe. The sheep picked the land clean along their path, preventing development of a substantial agriculture, devastating the land and perhaps causing a permanent change in the climate by the widespread destruction of vegetation. In many places it has not recovered in the one hundred years since the herds disappeared.

The plaza at Garovillas has a handsome two level portico on three sides, a reminder of the days when the plaza served as the bull ring and the upper story viewing spaces were in demand. It now hosts a small market for several hours every morning. Until a few years ago the well in the center was the only source of water for the neighborhood. A recently installed water system has eased the burden of carrying water and permitted the well to be replaced with an ugly, but 'up to date' terrazzo structure. Much of the cobble paving has also been replaced by concrete. Progress has its price (94-96, 19).

The Portugese gained independence from the Moors in the twelfth century, emerged as a world power in the fifteenth, were eclipsed in the sixteenth but have remained more or less independent, if somewhat impoverished, ever since. While political separation from Spain encouraged the development of a distinctive vernacular architecture, the pervasive influence of Iberian history, geography, and climate determined that it would be a variation on the basic Iberian themes, not a radical departure.

Though the Mediterranean influence is felt throughout the peninsula, the farther removed from the eastern and southern coasts, the less intense it is, until in the far north and northwest it disappears almost entirely (helped, undoubtedly by the cool, wet un-Mediterranean climate). Portugal shares some of this remoteness, though not as conspicuously as the north of Spain. In addition Portugal, like Spain, was a maritime power, with colonies all over the world. This contact with other cultures was felt at home, though little filtered into the remote rural areas.

There are other differences that one senses immediately on entering from Spain into Portugal. Life slows down perceptibly. The towns are quieter and cleaner; the twentieth century is much less in evidence. Compared with Spain's headlong rush to modernize, Portugal is proceeding much more slowly and less destructively --exemplified by the superb preservation of Monsaraz (106-116), one of the most beautiful villages in Iberia.

The photograph on page 93 is of wine caves dug in a low hill near Benavente.

NORTHERN IBERIA

As the photographs reveal, there is considerable justification in dividing so complex a land as Iberia into simply 'north' and 'south'. The logic derives, in part, from the differences in geography and climate (the cool, rainy north versus the hot, dry south), in part, from cultural differences (northern Christianity versus southern Islam), and in part, from architectural antecedents as diverse as the medieval towns of northern Europe and the casbahs of North Africa.

The two regions also share architectural characteristics. Most evident is the Mediterranean influence along the coasts particularly in the south with its more Mediterranean-like climate. In addition, the basic need for accessibility to water and agricultural land, and for defendable sites led to the building of towns on hilltops in both the north and south. And, though by no means uniform in their effect, the periodic dominance of a single culture over most of Iberia, such as the Romans, the Moors, and finally the Catholic Christians, also had a unifying influence.

The line dividing northern and southern vernacular is hardly precise. If I were to define such a line (no Spaniard or Portugese is likely to agree), it would begin at a point just above Valencia on the Mediterranean coast to below Madrid and Toledo in the center and end south of Lisbon on the Atlantic.

Naturally, a different physical environment leads to alternate house forms and construction techniques and general layout of the villages. Man does not merely adapt to a given environment; he changes it, principly through his buildings which moderate the given conditions into something suitable and comfortable. Out of these efforts, through imagination and reason, and the capacity to exchange ideas, man forges a building tradition --a language of form communicable to the whole society.

Materials

Iberian building materials are the same ones used throughout the Mediterranean --cut or rubble stone, rammed earth and adobe, wood for the walls and structure, and with tile, thatch, and slate for the roof. The most plentiful materials in a particular locality are the ones most likely to predominate but they are seldom used to the exclusion of all others. In fact one characteristic of Iberian vernacular is the easy combination of stone, adobe, and wood in a single structure.

Wood with its unique structural capabilities is nearly universal --sparingly used in the dry central and southern areas where it was scarce and the only fuel, but extensively in the forested northern mountains. Only wooden beams could easily span floors and roofs (65). Between the beams were laid small planks and twigs which were plastered over for floors or covered with thatch, tile, or slate for roofing. Wood framed walls, usually in the half-timber technique had larger vertical and horizontal members with an infill of stone rubble or 'wattle and daub' --a woven lattice of twigs plastered on both sides (85).

Perhaps the most typical material and the one that most frequently comes to mind in connection with this land is *pise de terre* - rammed earth and adobe. It is the one material readily at hand on every building site though its appropriateness in the rainy areas is questionable. Rammed earth walls are constructed on a foundation of stone from 6 inches to 2 feet in height to keep moisture out of the wall. Then, in a movable wooden form, dampened earth scooped up from nearby and mixed with straw, is packed in layers from 18 to 24 inches thick. The form slides along at each level and the process is repeated to the desired height. To protect the surface a thin layer of durable plaster is applied and over this frequent coats of whitewash provide a tough weatherproof surface. Though a torrential downpour of long duration can melt it away, such construction endures for generations with occasional surface renewal. In any case it is relatively easy to rebuild or extend.

A variation is adobe; blocks of mud mixed with straw hand molded or cast in a form and set in the sun to dry. The adobe is then piled up and plastered over in shapes similar to the rammed earth. Usually in these earthen buildings, the door and window frames and other areas subject to high wear or requiring precise fit are of stone or wood.

A similar variation is brick. Most often associated with the Mudejar or Muslim style, it may have been introdced then. To make bricks requires a good source of raw materials, kilns and a plentiful supply of fuel, so they were not as widely available as other materials.

Stone in various forms --rubble from river beds, limestone from surface quarries, and large boulders cleared from the fields --is another basic material. Rubble walls (plain or plastered) and shaped stones were combined in handsome and structurally ingenious ways (36-39, 43, 63). Advantage was taken even of huge boulders to form parts of houses or barns especially around Portugal's Monsanto (37).

Occasionally the choice of material, technique or form went beyond the established norms. Innovations were introduced by some exceptionally skilled craftsman or requested by an owner who wished to build a little grander, more distinctive home (64-65, 76-77), such as the home for a wealthy sheep rancher whose migratory herds brought him to a remote village. The changes were not extreme --a slight increase in scale, greater use of an expensive material, and perhaps more lavish decorative elements, but the tradition was changed and expanded nevertheless.

Ancient Round Houses

While most houses are rectangular in plan, one of the most unusual northern houses is circular or oval. The type may be descended from the round houses discovered in the ancient *castros* of the Iberians and Celtics.

Simple, but effective shelter, the *pallaza*, as they are known, appear to have changed little over the centuries (46-48). The oval shape, efficient to build and heat, was divided into two sections by a central masonry wall with the stable usually on the north, and the family living quarters on the other side. The center of family life during the long winters was a large open hearth surrounded by benches. Hanging above the fire was a chain from which were hung cooking pots or meat for smoking. The natural earth floor, packed hard from use and sealed with dung, sloped gradually towards the stable. There was only one door for both the family and the animals --it plus a few tiny windows were the only source of light so the interior was dark even at midday.

Villages composed of *pallazas* were small with only a few houses scattered over a hilltop.

The round shape did not lend itself to compact grouping and there was always the danger of fire spreading in the thatched roofs.

The sharing of living space by man and his animals was common in early societies. The animals contributed needed heat to the living space and as the family's most valuable possessions were kept secure. The lack of ventilation, must have been oppressive, however. A later solution with animals on the lower floor and the living space above, while it had some inconveniences, was a decided improvement (49-51).

Some of the best examples of this advanced house type are in the village of Carmona (49-51). Built primarily of stone, they are a common type in the north. Set between jutting stone walls in row-house fashion, the two-story houses invariably feature a sun gallery the full width of the upper living level. A cantilevered tiled roof shelters the balcony. Decoration is confined to carvings on the balcony railings, balustrades, and window frames. Recently these balconies, particularly in the towns, have been totally glassed in to make private solaria.

The lower floor, which houses the work, storage, and animal spaces, has a large arched opening into which the family cart can be driven. Rows of these houses with their arches and balconies begin to resemble the arcaded streets so numerous in northern towns.

Medieval Towns

In the western mountains of Spain is a group of villages unlike any others. Reminiscent of the busy medieval towns of northern Europe, their development in these remote wooded mountains is strange indeed. Premier among them, and now proclaimed a national treasure, is La Alberca (78-91). Built on a gentle slope unrestricted by walls or site, the extreme piling up of La Alberca's houses seems to have no practical foundation. More likely, it derives from an instinctive desire for mutual support and security so prevalent elsewhere in folk cultures and in the Mediterranean particularly. Surrounded by oak groves, La Alberca is an agricultural village and was once important for charcoal production.

The typical La Alberca house, similar to those in nearby villages, has some unusual characteristics. The house is narrow, deep front to back and several stories high. The ground floor contains an entrance hall, staircase to the upper floors and storage or stables. Sleeping rooms are on the intermediate floors with only tiny windows front and rear, and the upper floor (which might be the second to the fifth level) is the main living space. The kitchen is here, with a constantly smoldering fire on a huge stone slab set in the floor. Smoke drifts up through the chinks in the roof or through the huge hood with a horizontal grill on which are placed chestnuts for drying or meat to be smoked. The years of smoke blacken the whole ceilng -though the hoods, made of wood covered with clay, may be freshly white washed.

Small front windows look out over the street or at the neighbor's house a few feet away. In the early days, garbage was tossed down into the streets to be consumed by roaming pigs or goats or swept away by the rains. When the houses open onto an interior court at the rear, there is often a small balcony --the only light and airy space in the whole house. Though the upper floor is the most pleasant space in the

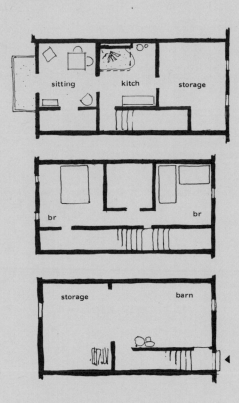

HOUSE, LA ALBERCA

house it was unending toil to haul up all the fuel, food, and water.

The houses of the La Alberca region combine stone, wood, and plaster. The lower walls and pillars are of massive stone -- sometimes with stone lintels --the upper floors are half-timber framing sealed with plaster.

In the narrow streets the projecting upper stories nearly shut out the light giving the towns a closed-in feeling with little sense of the sky above and the landscape beyond. The only large open spaces are plazas. Here and along major streets the houses incorporate porticos which join together in arcades for the gathering of the townspeople, for market stalls, and as extensions to the shops and work spaces.

Porticoed streets (66-67, 72-73, 94-96), a prominent feature in many northern towns, even though they darken the ground floor interiors (60-61), provide useful public spaces. The effect of a whole arcaded street or square is quite extraordinary and goes a long way to humanize the space. The portico is a relatively late development in Iberian vernacular, perhaps as recent as the fifteenth century. If true, the idea spread rapidly and widely. Considering the desirability of shade in southern towns, it seems strange the portico is seldom found.

With the few exceptions discussed above, northern villages when compared with southern villages tend to be more regular in their layout and less densely built-up. Streets are normally wider for more access to light and sun. However, when constricted by encircling walls or cliffs the towns grew vertically with multi-story houses (53, 75) and the streets became dark tunnels.

One of the few examples of pure decoration is patterned plaster known as sgraffito (73, 91). Used mainly in the Segovia region the geometric designs remind us of arabic patterns in the Alhambra of Granada. The technique consists of covering a colored layer of plaster with a light-colored layer, then with the aid of a stencil the top layer is scratched away to expose the colors. Finally the whole surface is burnished smooth.

A technical innovation in heating found in northern Castile is the gloria. It is based on a network of ducts beneath the floor through which passes the heat and smoke from a fire at one side of the house, warming the tiled floor in the process. Only the kitchen and living room floors are warmed. Firewood is scarce so straw is burned in a closed firepit so that it smolders through the night while the adobe and tile mass retains the heat for hours. In the summer a natural draft cools the floors.

Whether handed down from Roman times or developed by a local craftsman to please a wealthy client, the gloria system spread, as its advantages became known, and became a part of the local building tradition. It is an example of how climate, human need, and available materials can be integrated into architectural form.

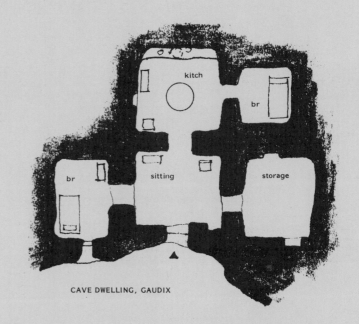

CAVE DWELLING, GAUDIX

SOUTHERN IBERIA

The most ancient houses still in use are southern cave dwellings. It is astounding to think that some of these caves may have been lived in continuously for thousands of years -- perhaps since the first Iberians 20,000 years ago. Natural caves or rock strata in which men carved out habitations for themselves are frequent in the south.

Cave Dwellings

Today we are rediscovering advantages in underground living, such as the constant temperature of the surrounding earth that keeps the interiors cool in summer and warm in winter. Since wood as fuel became scarce long ago, this advantage was not lost on the early cave dwellers. An obvious disadvantage, the lack of light and air, was minimized by ingenious light and ventilation shafts plus generous use of whitewash inside and out to reflect the light deep into the interiors.

Set in a surreal landscape punctuated with white chimneys, the most dramatic cave community is Gaudix (126-129). Chimneys and whitewashed doorways are the only clues to the maze of rooms that honeycombs the soft, eroded stone.

More typical are underground dwellings similar to those at La Guardia pass. Here the earth has been dug out to form rooms and the hill side carved into a flat facade and patio. Every surface is whitewashed to seal and preserve it. A superb integration of man-made and natural forms, it is also an example of man's need, even though he makes his home in the ground, to define a personal space that contrasts with nature. Here the demarcation is through the abstract clarity of the severe, white surfaces.

Compare the grass-roofed cave of La Guardia with the rare example of a thatched roof house (24) -- the relation of roof to wall is remarkably similar. In fact the La Guardia caves can, on first glance, be mistaken for thatched houses.

The cave dwellings at Setenil (130-134) go a step further by up-to-date additions of conventional facades covering the original caves set in the cliffs of the river bank. Situated high, dry and secure, the spectacular cliff dwelling near Monte Frio (177) is another cave that probably has been occupied for eons.

In all of these cave houses the layouts are limited by the sheer labor of making the spaces and the decreasing light and air as one penetrates further into the ground. Typical cave dwellings open initially into a large room which is the main living space with subsidiary spaces branching off in petal fashion. The cooking usually is done in a separate space with its own chimney or outside in good weather.

A more conventional southern house is one of simple stone and adobe blocks found all over in the country towns. The shapes are elemental but in combination they achieve wondrously complex forms and spaces (138, 160). Despite the south's Islamic traditions, these houses seldom have interior courts. They are too small and in the country towns there is less need to escape the press of urban life. Instead the streets, tiny plazas or walled-in yards provide the outdoor living spaces.

Patio Houses

The most elaborate and best known type, the patio house, is based on Islamic concepts. It is the typical house in the larger more sophisticated towns where there was a stronger Islamic influence and a greater need for privacy.

SOUTHERN IBERIA
PHOTOGRAPHS

The southern Portugese village of Monsaraz
(106-116) is one of the most attractive villages in Iberia
and seems destined to remain so as it is now under
government protection. Despite this control it is filled
with the normal activities of a living town. As such it is
an example of how the Iberian traditional village can
incorporate new standards of living and new
technology without destroying its very fabric.
    The site, on a hill overlooking the Spanish border,
explains the need for walls and castle.

    A composition of traditional forms. Albufeira (105).

Monsaraz´s main street and plaza (108-109).

In this view (110) we look from the front door on the street through the main living space, with its slate floor and simple furniture, into the private patio in the rear. The few possessions are stored in several niches in the walls.

Monsaraz epitomizes the differences between Portugese and Spanish villages. In Portugal the pace is slower, the towns seem cleaner, and, if it is possible, more freshly whitewashed. And everywhere much less evidence of a frantic modernization.

This room is just inside the front door. A sitting room is off to the left, kitchen through the door at the rear, and sleeping rooms are up the stair. It is spotlessly clean, beautifully simple and elegant. Difficult though it may be to believe, this house, like the one on page 110, is typical Portugese vernacular in daily use by a family, not a room set up in a museum (115).

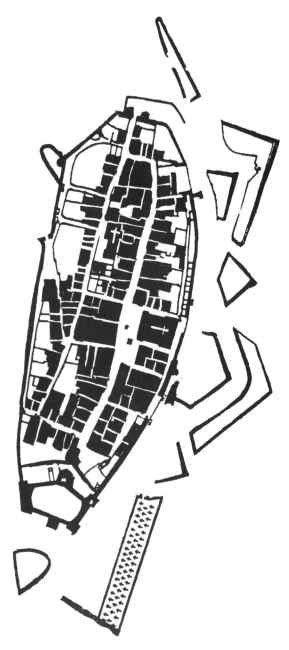

SCALE 1:2500

Textures of Monsaraz roofs and paving set off by the white walls (116).

Mertola, Portugal (117). Comparing this town and Monsaraz with the Spanish towns of Casares (152) and Monte Frio (178) demonstrates the related but differing character in both the individual buildings and the townscape of Portugese and Spanish towns.

Calcadinha, outside Elvas, is a one street town centered on the gate of the landowner's estate (118). The row houses with their imposing chimneys and sculpted terraces are at Terrugem (119, 121t).

One of the fascinations in traveling through southern Portugal is the study of the inventive chimney forms — no two are alike. These are in the Loule area (120, 121b).

Evocative symbols of La Mancha, these windmills on a ridge above Consuegra face the constant winds of the waterless plains (manxa is the arabic word for parched earth). The castle was a 12th century outpost between the Islamic and Christian territories manned by knights who were rewarded with grazing rights over this vast region. Windmills testify to its later transformation into a grain producing area.

Equally symbolic of the south are the whitewashed wall and tile roof. The detail shows traditional roof tiles and the ridge capped with layered tiles, mortared in place and sealed with whitewash.

The south has some unexpected building types
— thatched roofs and underground houses. The soft
earth, hollowed out and whitewashed, makes efficient
living spaces — warm in winter and cool in summer.
Though windows are small, the whitewash inside and
out reflects light deep inside. Near Utrera (124). La
Guardia (125).

This surreal scene of moonscape pierced by strange white forms is Guadix, a large community of underground houses near Granada (126-128).

Marked only by their whitewashed chimneys and entrances, these houses extend under the whole area in a warren of spaces carved out of the earth. This place has been occupied since pre-historic times probably in much the same way. Cave house with red peppers hung to dry near Baza (129).

Setenil began as a series of ancient cave dwellings burrowed into the cliffs along the river. A conventional town has since grown up around and the caves, still very much in use, have been expanded with conventional fronts (130-134).

Olvera's image sticks in the mind long after leaving. It is uncommonly beautiful, whether when first seen from many miles away gleaming on its hill top in the midst of great rolling plains of olive groves, or more closely, with its houses rippling down between the rocks like a giant glacier issuing from the cathedral. It is a wedding of townscape and landscape that enobles each — and easy to imagine the inhabitants' pride in such a place (135-137).

Of the many tranquil villages near Ronda, several
just south of the town are especially beautiful. Small
country towns set in wooded hills, their modest houses,
churches and winding streets are immaculate with every
wall freshly whitewashed. As in most southern towns,
during the day the streets are deserted except for an
occasional solitary figure venturing into the hot sun.
Alpandere (138-143).

Composed of simple elements and materials,
Alpandere shows how a rich environment may be
unconsciously created in a small village. The dwellings
are strung along the spines and gentle slopes of the low
hills connected by a complex network of streets and tiny
plazas — spaces enhanced by changing, contrapuntal
patterns of light and shade. And always, just beyond,
is the green unspoiled landscape.

Vejer de la Frontera is a compact hilltown whose
narrow winding streets invite wandering — especially
in the cool evening when doorways are left ajar for
intriguing glimpses of flower-adorned interior patios.
A legacy of the Moslem period, these private spaces on
which most rooms open, give each house access to sun
and air despite the narrow streets (144-145, 15).

144

*A southern landscape with olive groves near
Bednar (146) and the castle town of Biar (147).*

One of Spain's most impressive castles soars above this white but dusty town. Velez Blanco's unpaved streets and rows of simple houses are typical of this barren area (148-150).

The random assembly of these austere forms delineated by the dark tile can create striking rhythms — patterns that are at once simple yet complex, clear yet ambiguous. Torre Alhaquime — a name of obvious Arabic antecedence (151).

Casares, the most spectacular of the white towns, has remained so because it was nearly inaccessible until recently and merited no mention in Baedekers. Perhaps inspired by the horrible example of other coastal towns such as Mijas now totally destroyed by rampant tourism, Casares will retain its fragile beauty (152-161).

At the very top is the town cemetary — above-ground vaults piled high in the limited space (153-154).

These spellbinding views of Casares compel reflection that alternates between the abstract geometry enhanced by the contrasting roofs, the sensuous textures of the weathered walls and tile, and the reality — suddenly verified by tiny figures who appear in their midst.

Ardales is a small Andalusian farming community, out of the way and little corrupted by too rapid change. Despite a fairly regular street layout, the random adaptation of the standard house form to the variations of the site has produced an exceedingly complex series of stepped rhythms up the hillside. The practical need to seal the ridges and exposed end walls with whitewashed tile emphasizes the pattern by outlining each roof plane in white. The underlying purpose may be practical but the inhabitants are not unaware of its aesthetic effects (162-167).

162

Ardales is another example, if one is needed, of how a village composed of simple elements can, by the uniqueness of its site and scale, achieve a distinctive character, and how practical solutions to construction details can add integral, even exuberant, decoration. These villages are composed of the same fundamental building types but the details and the relationships of the parts are infinitely variable so that each village, each street, each plaza is unique yet familiar.

Ardales is in many ways the archetypal Andalusian village — white houses on a hillside beneath a ruined castle, surrounded by olive trees as far as the eye can see.

Problems of security, scarcity of water, and the system of land ownership have limited isolated farms to only a few areas. These compounds of houses and barns are in the exceptionally green and beautiful Valle de Abdalgis between Alora and Antequera (168-169).

In the middle of fragrant orange and lemon groves is this large farm compound near Alora — complete with its own chapel (170-171). The owner now lives in town and the manager's family occupies a portion of the house. Included in the compound are stables, a giant olive press and a large kitchen (171b) with a huge hood over the former cooking area.

To keep the interiors cool in summer and warm in winter the windows are few and small; however, the combination of shutters, splayed walls, and whitewash softens the glare from the sun outside and diffuses its light throughout the interior.

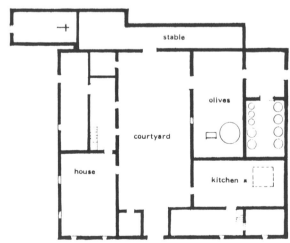

The village of Atajate near Ronda steps down the south slope so each house catches the sun and view. It is unusual because, except for the tower, its church is built in the same style as the houses. The result is a tiny village of unified composition that sits elegantly in the unspoiled landscape unmarred even by the, at times oppressive, mass of a church (172-173).

El Burgo, whose roof patterns are another and
distinctive variation on the Andalusian theme (174).

In the towns projecting window bays allow
discrete views up and down the street yet maintain
privacy for the women of the house — similar to the
shuttered balconies in the old Moslem towns in Africa.
Their irregular repetition along the facades accented by
the black grill work adds a striking sculptural effect
to these plain walls in Ronda (175).

In the mountains near Granada where the last Arabs held out, a unique style persists that is remarkably similar to houses in the Atlas mountains of Morocco. The roofs are flat, made of layers of mud, and used for food and clothes drying. The upper stories often incorporate loggias — outdoor living spaces oriented to the sun and view. Near Orjiva (176t). Capileira (176b).

This cliff dwelling near Monte Frio undoubtedly has an ancient history, for such places were the first homes of man in this area. The upper entrance is the house — whitewashed and terraced to lend it a certain dignity — the other entrances are to storage rooms (177).

Through this cleft in the hills the first glimpse of Monte Frio's jewel white forms against the olive green backdrop is breathtaking. The combination of natural and man-made forms culminates in the perfectly sited fortress church. Walled off at the lower end, this central rock around which wrap the older sections of the town was Monte Frio's natural castle to which the townspeople could retreat in times of crisis.

Like Monsaraz and Casares, Monte Frio is a vital
place demonstrating how people cling to village life if
they are able to enjoy minimal modern conveniences
and find work nearby. Thankfully bypassed by the
crass tourism that has destroyed so many Iberian
towns, Monte Frio, not only in its overall aspects but in
many of its details, remains an authentic and inspiring
example of Iberian vernacular.

The desire for privacy and the need to both shade the summer sun and embrace it during the colder months led to exterior walls with small openings and rooms that opened onto interior patios. For ample sunlight most houses are not more than one or two stories especially if the court is small. The patio is filled with plants and flowers and may include a well or pool. It is the center of family life in good weather --a play space for children, the laundry and kitchen, a work space, and a gathering spot for evening relaxation. Despite the extremely narrow streets and the solidly packed houses, the low patio house kept the overall density to less than some medieval towns of the north.

One reason the smaller villages lacked the sophisticated patio house is that Islam is an urban phenomenon. Towns grew up around the markets surrounding the main mosque. The market or suq, held weekly, was essential to the economy of a large area and sometimes the very reason for a towns's existence. One still finds these weekly markets in rural Spain, Portugal, Mexico and most of the Arab world. Country folk came from miles around to buy and sell their goods and attend the Friday mosque, --one reason the markets were often held on that day.

Markets may have originated in the town center but the need for larger and larger areas as the town grew caused their shift to the outskirts --just inside or outside the walls near the main gates. The site for festivals and even bull fights, many plaza mayors owe their existence to those early markets.

Most smaller towns have changed little since the reconquest. They are still a maze of streets, lined with introverted houses, interspersed with tiny plazas, all without

EPITAPH

Portent of the fate of vernacular architecture in Iberia and the world. Estepona (184t) and Villafuerte (184b).

apparent order. Unhindered by central planning and with little sense of community responsibility (the streets were merely a path to the tranquility of one's own home), the towns reflect adaptation to the interior forces of town life --a life of multiplicity as opposed to the renaissance ideal of centralized hierarchical order.

Gardens and Patios

I would like to comment on Iberian and Islamic gardens. In the grander, more formal gardens, the combined influence of Islam and the later infusion of a renaissance desire for order have resulted in an extraordinary insensitivity to plant forms. It is not at all unusual to see a scraggly tree set forlornly in the midst of a hard tile floor, or rigid rows of slowly dying shrubs, or discordant collections of ungainly plants as the main features of patios and court yards. The apparent desire for total geometric order created an unsympathetic, artificial environment for man or plants. In contrast, the intimate scale of the private patios and the casual arrangements of abundant flowers and shrubs in pots on the floors, steps, sills or hung on the walls creates a humane and inviting atmosphere.(141, 144-145).

The insensitivity to domesticated plants may stem from a background in the waterless environment of the Arabian Peninsula and North Africa. One gets the sense that the survival of any growing thing, no matter how pathetic, is a triumph of man over environment. The sympathetic relation of plants and architecture of Japan, for example, would be incomprehensible. The walled garden represents the control of man over nature -- perhaps in response to the harsh realities of the world outside that space.

Nearly every patio or court includes a fountain, well, or pool. The water was present not only for daily use but also for its psychological effects -the sense of coolness and movement in the enervating heat.

The White Towns

The most spectacular southern villages are, of course, the white hilltowns. Most have now disappeared, buried under tourist hotels and condominiums that litter the Iberian coasts. It is safe to say, that from the French border to the Algarve in Portugal any village within a few miles of the coast is no longer worth visiting and the whole coast so dreary as to make one wonder why anyone still bothers.

Thankfully, some outstanding hilltowns remain in the interior, though one hesitates to identify their locations. Ardales, Olvera, Monte Frio, and especially Casares in Spain and Monsaraz in Portugal. After the desecration of the coast, to visit these brilliant towns is a reminder that man at one time was capable of making an environment of great beauty, sympathetic to nature and himself --and that he may still do so again.

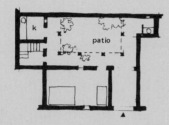

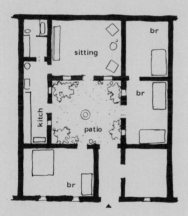

PATIO HOUSES

...the vernacular architecture of farms and inns and the narrow streets of little villages, that is not really architecture at all from an academic point of view, but just the straight forward instinctive building of grave and kindly men behind whom lies the creative tradition of two thousand years.

...here is the art of building reduced to its simplest and plainest forms, and ...is a wholesome lesson for architects of small things (actually more vital and important than the big things) and is a stimulus and inspiration as well.

Consider the simplicity of the materials and forms. Rough rubble, either left grey and silvery or washed a thousand times with white...brown natural wood, and rough tiles of every possible shade...There is little brick and less cut stone, while ornament is most sparingly used; a roughly carved capital here and there, a door architrave, a coat of arms, there is little more, and the effect comes from instinctively good proportions, a perfect designing and placing of windows, and a picturesqueness of composition that is so good it could not be premeditated. The Spaniard understands the wall and roof as no one else: he can build up his flat wall of rubble, cover it with a toned white wash, pierce it with a door and a few windows, add a balcony and two 'rijas', crown the whole with a sweeping roof of tawny tiles, plant two cypress and an almond nearby, and produce a composition that is the despair of the trained and cultured architect...

Pictures such as these are for students and creators of the real architecture of a people; not for copying, but for mental and spiritual illumination...

Ralph Adams Cram, Architect
Boston, 1923

BIBLIOGRAPHY AND NOTES

Architectura popular em Portugal. (2 vols). Lisbon: National Union of Architects, 1961.

Baedeker, K. *Spain and Portugal.* Stuttgart, 1959.

3   Brennan, G. *The Spanish Labyrinth.* London 1943.

2   Dubos, Rene. *So Human an Animal.* New York: Scribners, 1968.

Echague, Jose Oritz. *Pueblos Y Paisajes.* Madrid 1966.

Feduchi, Luis. *Arquitectura Popular Espanola.* Barcelona: Editorial Blume, 1975 (5 vols).

Flores, Carlos. *Arquitectura Popular Espanola.* Madrid: Aguilar, 1973.

1   Gutkind, E. A. *Urban development in Southern Europe: Spain and Portugal. International History of City Development, Vol III.* New York: The Free Press, 1967.

Michener, James A. *Iberia.* New York: Random House, 1968.

Mumford, Lewis. *The City in History.* New York: Harcourt, Brace and World, 1961.

Morris, James. *The Presence of Spain.* New York: Harcourt, Brace, and World, 1964.

INDEX

References to photographs are in ( ).

IBERIA

CANGAS
SANTILLANA
CARMONA
GOIZUETA
● SANTIAGO DE C
EL CEBRERO
FRIAS   VINUESA
PENALBA DE SANTIAGO
ACEBO

LINDOSO
BENEVENTE
PENARANDA DE DUERO
BRAGA
VILLAFUERTE
● BARCELONA

BATEA
HORTA

PEDRAZA
SEGOVIA

MORELLA
GUARDA
LA ALBERCA
ALCALA
MIRANDA
● MADRID
VALBONA
MONSANTO
CUENCA
LA GUARDIA

GAROVILLAS
VALENCIA

CONSUEGRA

ALMANSA
LISBON
TERRUGEM
BIAR
CALCADINHA

MONSARAZ

BEDNAR

MERTOLA
VELEZ BLANCO
BAZA
● SEVILLA
MONTE FRIO
GAUDIX
LOULE
UTRERA
● GRANADA
CAPILEIRA
ALBUFEIRA
OLVERA
ARDALES   ABDALGIS
TORRE
ALORA
ORJIVA
SETENIL
EL BURGO
RONDA
ALPANDERE
VEJER
ATAJATE
CASARES
CASTELLAR
ESTEPONA

PHOTOGRAPHIC NOTES

The photographs are the result of seven trips to Spain and Portugal since 1970. Because of the tremendous variety in the photographs it was difficult to make the final selection. The book could easily have been twice the size --but alas, twice the price.

There is always a let-down when I finish my travels in a country. I no longer have the excuse to return to some unexplored corner or to re-photograph a favorite village under different light. Some places give one a feeling of relief when you have quit them, but Spain and Portugal still fascinate and I am sure I will return.

The photographs were made with Hasselblad cameras using lenses from 38 to 500mm. Also used were 35mm Nikon and Olympus cameras with lenses from 21 to 200mm. Most of the photographs were duplicated in color. The black and white, however, always took precedence. For me they are the most compelling and being the most abstract, are the strongest images.

AVAILABILITY OF PRINTS:
Archival prints made by Norman F. Carver, Jr. are available of any photograph in the book. A portfolio of 10 prints is also available. Prices as of 1981 range from $50 to $200 per print depending on size. For current prices please contact the photographer in care of the publisher, Documan Press, Box 387, Kalamazoo, Michigan 49005, USA.